I0825152

TO

____

FROM

____

DATE

____

JUST THINK,

you're here not by chance
but by God's choosing.
His hand formed you
and made you the person you are.
He compares you to no one else—
you are one of a kind.
You lack nothing
that His grace can't give you.
He has allowed you to be here
at this time in history
to fulfill His special purpose
for this generation.

—ROY LESSIN

PROVERBS 16:24

KIND WORDS ARE LIKE HONEY SWEET TO THE SOUL

JOURNAL

Love your enemies, do good to them,
and lend to them without expecting to get anything back.
Then your reward will be great.

LUKE 6:35 NIV

Encouragement is awesome. It can actually change the course of another person's day, week, or life.

CHUCK SWINDOLL

Love is patient and kind. Love is not jealous or boastful or proud or rude. It does not demand its own way.

I CORINTHIANS 13:4–5 NLT

I believe He wants us to love others
so much that we go to extremes to help them.

FRANCIS CHAN

Be kind to one another, tenderhearted, forgiving one another, as God in Christ forgave you.

EPHESIANS 4:32 ESV

Nothing is so strong as gentleness,
nothing so gentle as real strength.

SAINT FRANCIS DE SALES

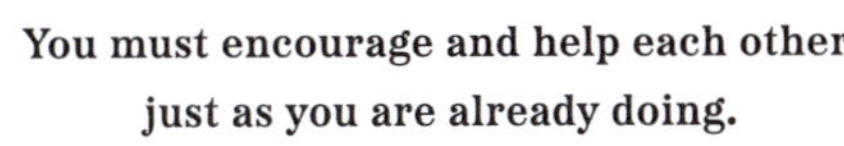

You must encourage and help each other, just as you are already doing.

I THESSALONIANS 5:11 CEV

If people can be taught to hate,
they can be taught to love! We must find the way,
you and I, no matter how long it takes.

CORRIE TEN BOOM

Worry weighs a person down;
an encouraging word cheers a person up.

PROVERBS 12:25 NLT

Every day may not be good,
but there's something good in every day.

ALICE MORSE EARLE

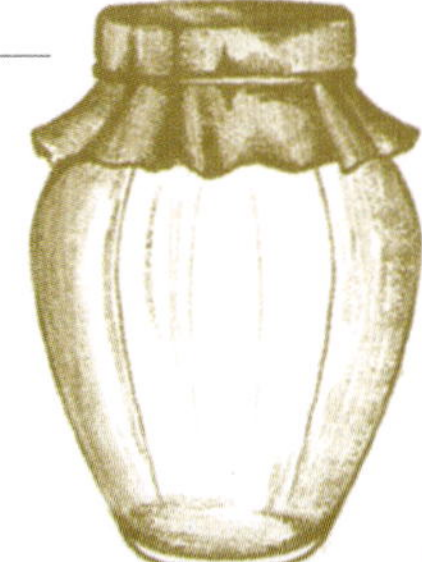

He did not leave Himself without witness, in that He did good,
gave us rain from heaven and fruitful seasons,
filling our hearts with food and gladness.

ACTS 14:17 NKJV

God doesn't start out tasting like tutti-frutti
and end up tasting like stinky socks....
Love is good and love tastes like good.

CATHERINE TOON

Therefore, as God's chosen people, holy and dearly loved, clothe yourselves with compassion, kindness, humility, gentleness and patience.

COLOSSIANS 3:12 NIV

**Compassion is willing to make sacrifices,
allows plans to be interrupted,
and is ready to be a part of the solution.**

CHRISTINE CAINE

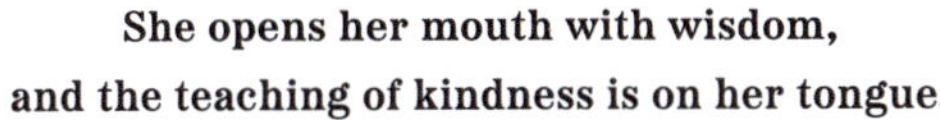

She opens her mouth with wisdom,
and the teaching of kindness is on her tongue.

PROVERBS 31:26 ESV

Wisdom should be what beckons us to speak—
it always raises others up with images of a better way.
Wise women are a gift to culture!

LISA BEVERE

God's Spirit makes us loving, happy, peaceful,
patient, kind, good, faithful, gentle, and self-controlled.
There is no law against behaving in any of these ways.

GALATIANS 5:22–23 CEV

The prayers we weave into the matching of socks,
the stirring of oatmeal, the reading of stories,
they survive fire.

ANN VOSKAMP

Whatever you wish that others would do to you, do also to them.

MATTHEW 7:12 ESV

How far you go in life depends on your being tender with the young, compassionate with the aged, sympathetic with the striving, and tolerant of the weak and strong. Because someday in your life you will have been all of these.

GEORGE WASHINGTON CARVER

We must help the weak,
remembering the words the Lord Jesus Himself said:
"It is more blessed to give than to receive."

ACTS 20:35 NIV

The more you give, the more comes back to you, because God is the greatest giver in the universe, and He won't let you outgive Him. Go ahead and try. See what happens.

RANDY ALCORN

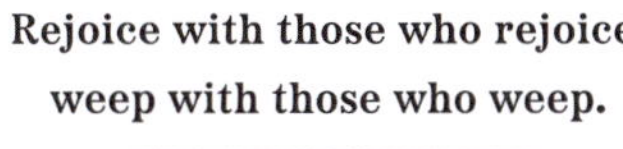

Rejoice with those who rejoice,
weep with those who weep.

ROMANS 12:15 ESV

When life is sweet, say thank You and celebrate.
And when life is bitter, say thank You and grow.

SHAUNA NIEQUIST

Pursue righteousness, godliness, faith, love, steadfastness, gentleness.

I TIMOTHY 6:11 ESV

Joy is the serious business of heaven.

C. S. LEWIS

He has shown you. . . . what is good;
and what does the LORD require of you but to do justly,
to love mercy, and to walk humbly with your God?

MICAH 6:8 NKJV

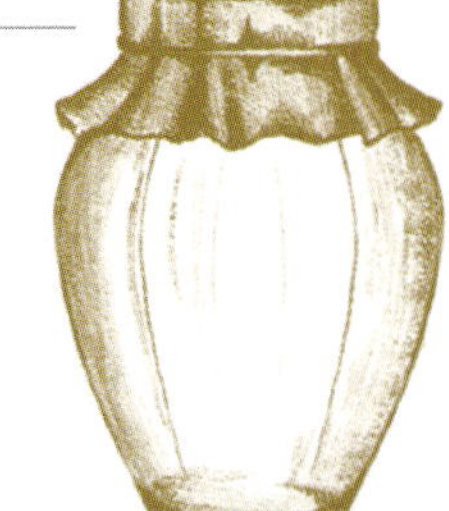

Generous giving begins
with the posture of total humility.

GORDON MACDONALD

Kind words are like honey—
they cheer you up and make you feel strong.

PROVERBS 16:24 CEV

Cold words freeze people, and hot words scorch them, and bitter words make them bitter, and wrathful words make them wrathful. Kind words also produce their image on men's souls; and a beautiful image it is. They smooth, and quiet, and comfort the hearer.

BLAISE PASCAL

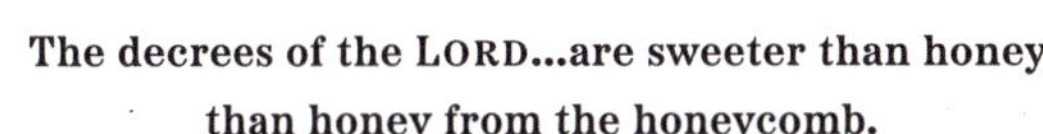

The decrees of the LORD...are sweeter than honey,
than honey from the honeycomb.

PSALM 19:9–10 NIV

The sound of "gentle stillness"
after all the thunder and wind have passed
will be the ultimate word from God.

JIM ELLIOT

Let your gentleness be evident to all.

PHILIPPIANS 4:5 NIV

Gentleness is an active trait, describing the manner in which we should treat others. Meekness is a passive trait, describing the proper Christian response when others mistreat us.

JERRY BRIDGES

Be completely humble and gentle; be patient,
bearing with one another in love. Make every effort to keep
the unity of the Spirit through the bond of peace.

EPHESIANS 4:2–3 NIV

The only way to practice peacemaking is to do the dang thing, step into the fray, speak with grace seasoned with salt, and fly the banner of the Prince of Peace!

AARTI SEQUEIRA

Do not be conformed to this world, but be transformed by the renewal of your mind, that by testing you may discern what is the will of God, what is good and acceptable and perfect.

ROMANS 12:2 ESV

You cannot expect to have peace around you if you do not have peace within you.

DR. TONY EVANS

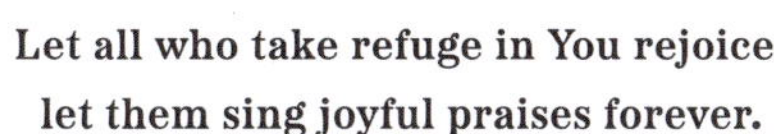

Let all who take refuge in You rejoice;
let them sing joyful praises forever.

PSALM 5:11 NLT

There is no virtue in the Christian life which is not made radiant with joy; there is no circumstance and no occasion which is not illuminated with joy. A joyless life is not a Christian life, for joy is one constant recipe for Christian living.

WILLIAM BARCLAY

We are His workmanship, created in Christ Jesus for good works, which God prepared beforehand so that we would walk in them.

EPHESIANS 2:10 NASB1995

We do good deeds,
but God works in us in the doing of them.

AUGUSTINE

Let nothing be done through selfish ambition or conceit,
but in lowliness of mind let each esteem others better than himself.

PHILIPPIANS 2:3 NKJV

He measures our lives by how we love.

FRANCIS CHAN

Be merciful, just as your Father is merciful.

LUKE 6:36 NIV

Remember that even Jesus' most scathing denunciation— a blistering diatribe against the religious leaders of Jerusalem in Matthew 23—ends with Christ weeping over Jerusalem. Compassion colored everything He did.

JOHN MACARTHUR

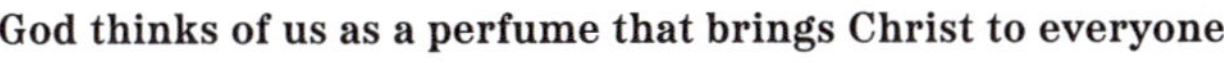

God thinks of us as a perfume that brings Christ to everyone.

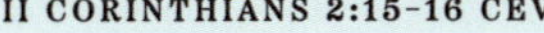

II CORINTHIANS 2:15-16 CEV

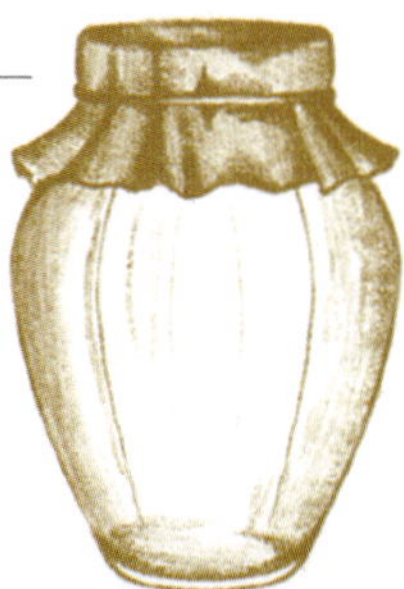

Too often we underestimate the power of a touch,
a smile, a kind word, a listening ear,
an honest compliment, or the smallest act of caring,
all of which have the potential to turn a life around.

LEO BUSCAGLIA

The meek will inherit the land and enjoy peace and prosperity.

PSALM 37:11 NIV

Sometimes the happiest ending isn't the one you keep longing for, but something you absolutely cannot see from where you are.

SHAUNA NIEQUIST

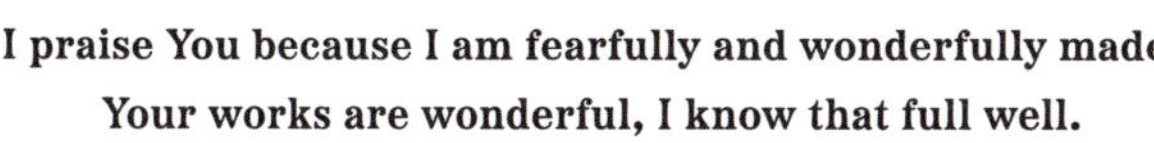
I praise You because I am fearfully and wonderfully made;
Your works are wonderful, I know that full well.

PSALM 139:14 NIV

Grace is God loving, God stooping,
God coming to the rescue, God giving Himself
generously in and through Jesus Christ.

JOHN STOTT

Do everything with love.

I CORINTHIANS 16:14 NLT

I cannot even imagine where I would be today were it not for that handful of friends who have given me a heart full of joy. Let's face it, friends make life a lot more fun.

CHUCK SWINDOLL

Let your roots grow down into Him, and let your lives be built on Him.
Then your faith will grow strong in the truth you were taught,
and you will overflow with thankfulness.

COLOSSIANS 2:7 NLT

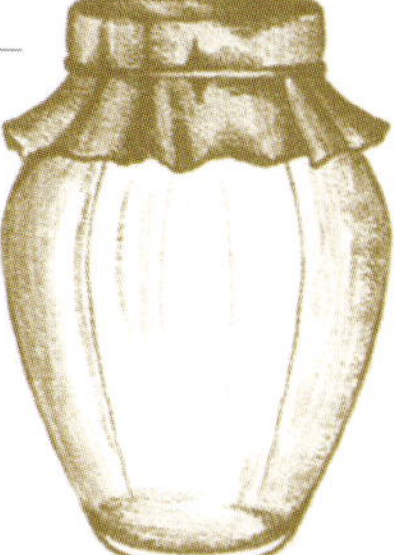

Our identity rests in God's relentless tenderness for us revealed in Jesus Christ.

BRENNAN MANNING

Kindness to the poor is a loan to the LORD,
and He will give a reward to the lender.

PROVERBS 19:17 CSB

To kindness and love, the things we need most!

THEODOR GEISEL (DR. SEUSS)

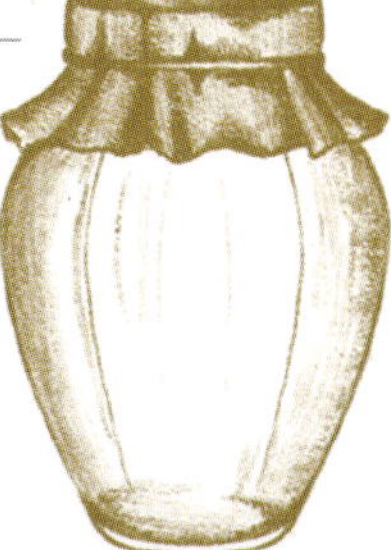

Be beautiful in your heart by being gentle and quiet.
This kind of beauty will last, and God considers it very special.

I PETER 3:4 CEV

Kindness makes a person attractive.
If you would win the world, melt it, do not hammer it.

ALEXANDER MACLAREN

A soft answer turns away wrath, but a harsh word stirs up anger.

PROVERBS 15:1 NKJV

No matter what good truths you have to teach,
no one will thank you if you do not speak kindly.

C. H. SPURGEON

Be gentle and show true humility to everyone.

TITUS 3:2 NLT

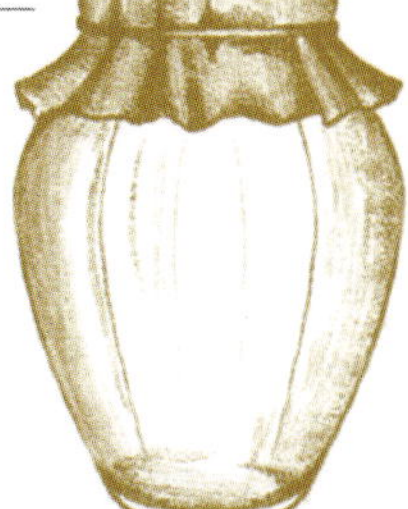

Gentleness says, "I will fight God's wars God's way. I can trust that His way of graciousness is right without resorting to manipulation or intimidation."

RANDY SMITH

Love each other with genuine affection, and take delight in honoring each other.

ROMANS 12:10 NLT

Have you ever noticed how much of Christ's life was spent in doing kind things?

HENRY DRUMMOND

The wisdom that comes from heaven is first of all pure;
then peace-loving, considerate, submissive,
full of mercy and good fruit, impartial and sincere.

JAMES 3:17 NIV

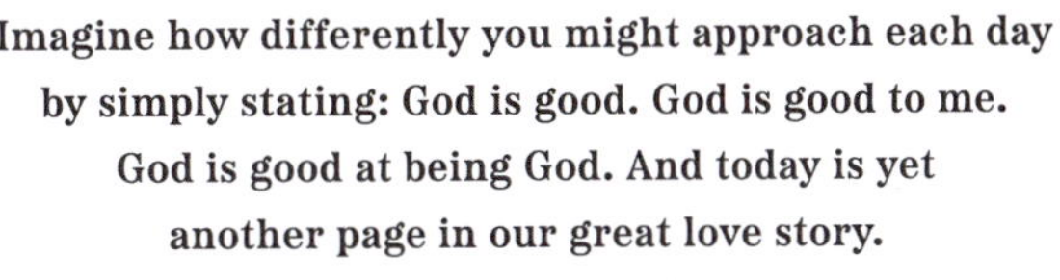

Imagine how differently you might approach each day by simply stating: God is good. God is good to me. God is good at being God. And today is yet another page in our great love story.

LYSA TERKEURST

God blesses those people who make peace.
They will be called His children!

MATTHEW 5:9 CEV

When our lives are filled with peace, faith, and joy, people will want to know what we have.

DAVID JEREMIAH

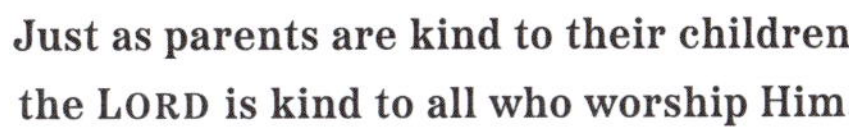

Just as parents are kind to their children,
the LORD is kind to all who worship Him.

PSALM 103:13 CEV

Let no one ever come to you without leaving better and happier. Be the living expression of God's kindness: kindness in your face, kindness in your eyes, kindness in your smile.

MOTHER TERESA

Blessed be the God and Father of our Lord Jesus Christ,
the Father of mercies and God of all comfort,
who comforts us in all our affliction, so that we may be able
to comfort those who are in any affliction, with the comfort
with which we ourselves are comforted by God.

II CORINTHIANS 1:3-4 ESV

Snuggle in God's arms. When you are hurting, when you feel lonely, left out, let Him cradle you, comfort you, reassure you of His all-sufficient power and love.

KAY ARTHUR

When the kindness and love of God our Savior appeared, He saved us, not because of righteous things we had done, but because of His mercy.

TITUS 3:4-5 NIV

Nothing is won by force. I choose to be gentle.
If I raise my voice, may it be only in praise.
If I clench my fist, may it be only in prayer.
If I make a demand, may it be only of myself.

MAX LUCADO

You will show me the way of life,
granting me the joy of Your presence
and the pleasures of living with You forever.

PSALM 16:11 NLT

Seek to cultivate a buoyant, joyous sense
of the crowded kindnesses of God in your daily life.

ALEXANDER MACLAREN

Let us therefore make every effort to do what leads to peace and to mutual edification.

ROMANS 14:19 NIV

God's peace flooded my soul, and my fear melted away.

ROSA PARKS

I tell you, love your enemies. Help and give without expecting a return. You'll never—I promise—regret it. Live out this God-created identity the way our Father lives toward us, generously and graciously, even when we're at our worst. Our Father is kind; you be kind.

LUKE 6:36 THE MESSAGE

Do all the good you can, by all the means you can,
in all the ways you can, in all the places you can,
at all the times you can, to all the people you can,
as long as ever you can.

JOHN WESLEY

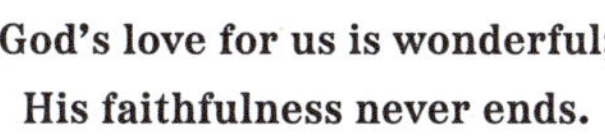

God’s love for us is wonderful;
His faithfulness never ends.

PSALM 117:2 CEV

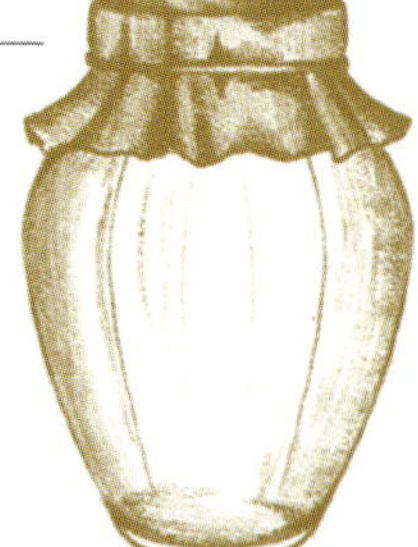

Good words are worth much, and cost little.

GEORGE HERBERT

The LORD, the LORD, the compassionate and gracious God,
slow to anger, abounding in love and faithfulness.

EXODUS 34:6 NIV

Love is the strongest force in the world.

CORRIE TEN BOOM

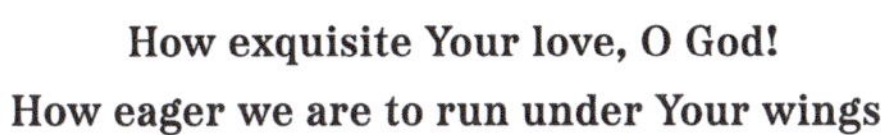

How exquisite Your love, O God!
How eager we are to run under Your wings.

PSALM 36:7 THE MESSAGE

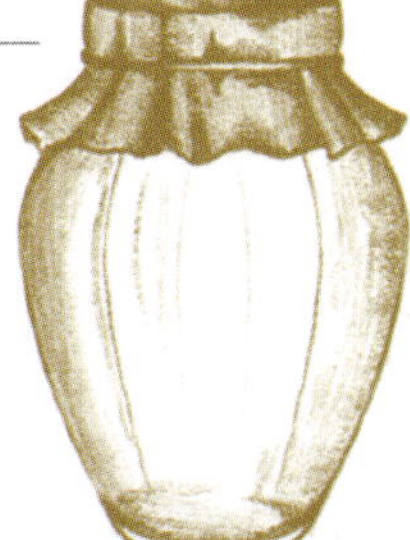

Be kind to yourself. God thinks you're worth His kindness.
And He's a good judge of character.

MAX LUCADO

Whoever goes hunting for what is right and kind finds life itself—*glorious* life!

PROVERBS 21:21 THE MESSAGE

In the darkest of nights cling to the assurance that God loves you, that He always has advice for you, a path that you can tread and a solution to your problem—and you will experience that which you believe. God never disappoints anyone who places his trust in Him.

BASILEA SCHLINK

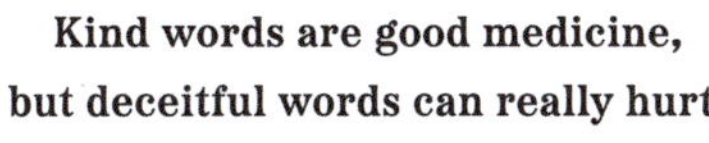

Kind words are good medicine,
but deceitful words can really hurt.

PROVERBS 15:4 CEV

Join me as I strive to cultivate a heart of kindness, to be tenderhearted and generous, and to lift up, encourage, affirm, love, support, bless, and comfort those who happen to cross my path.

CANDACE CAMERON BURE

Let your conversation be always full of grace, seasoned with salt, so that you may know how to answer everyone.

COLOSSIANS 4:6 NIV

Jesus says, *You want to know what to get Me as a present? Give me the love you say you have for Me, and transfer it. Touch the lives of others.*

DR. TONY EVANS

First Edition, March 2024

Published by:

21154 Highway 16 East
Siloam Springs, AR 72761
dayspring.com

Compilation by: Trieste Vaillancourt
Cover Design: Jenna Wilusz

Printed in China
Prime: J9602
ISBN: 978-1-64870-922-7